We all look forward to the World Cup, even if you are not actually going to be there. But there is a part of the championships that causes grown men to weep and young children to hide behind the sofa. Yes, it's **the opening ceremony.**

The first thing you notice about opening ceremonies is that the **commentators' voices** change. People more used to giving you statistics about the offside rule and talking you through the action replays, suddenly have to talk about dancing, doves, lines of happy children, people in weird outfits and all the rest of the vile gubbins that makes up the average opening ceremony. They go all serious, or start talking like your weird Uncle Norman. Their sentences   start   to   have   big   gaps   in between   the   words   because   they have   to   say   something   to fill   all   that   time.

All that time! That's the next thing you notice: these things go on for a very long time. There have been wars that have been shorter than the average opening ceremony. To overcome the tedium you will have to be prepared. If you are actually in the stadium, hard cheese buster, we can't do anything to help you (why did you buy a ticket when you knew you'd have to sit through the opening ceremony?). At home, however, you can rig up a bed in front of the TV, lay in plenty of supplies and wait until the all clear sounds.

Written and illustrated by
Martin Chatterton

PUFFIN BOOKS

Published by the Penguin Group: London, New York, Australia,
Canada, New Zealand, South Africa
Penguin Books Ltd, Registered Offices: Harmondsworth, Middlesex, England

First published 1998
1 3 5 7 9 10 8 6 4 2

Made and printed in Great Britain by William Clowes Ltd, Beccles and London

A CIP catalogue record for this book is available from the British Library

ISBN 0–141–30045–0

PUFFIN BOOKS

... and, with the big game about to start, it's over to our match commentators Gary Bloke and Retired Footballer.

OFF KICK KICK OFF

Thanks, Des. Well, we're getting used to the big occasions here on Channel Nutty, and they don't come much bigger than this one: the World Cup Finals! Let's get straight into the action. Here's how the Channel Nutty coverage is shaping up:

How does that line up strike you, Retired Footballer?

It's an attacking formation obviously. I think you'll see plenty of nonsense right through the book with complete rubbish coming from all directions! You can also expect to see New Nutty World Cup Rules and Nutty World Cup Facts getting forward to support the front two. The Nutty World Cup Quiz has been given a free role, sitting in front of midfield.

Thanks, Retired.

The Doves/Balloons. Every opening ceremony has either a flock of doves being released or a load of balloons. It can be quite good fun if they release both at the same time but this unfortunately doesn't happen often. We recommend taking a few large birds of prey along under your coat and releasing them at the same time as the doves, to add a bit of spice to the occasion.

The Silly Costumes. Usually these are connected in some way to a bit of history relevant to the country in which the finals are being played. For instance, for a final played in Italy we would get a few Romans and some arty medieval types. In England it would be some knights in armour. In France it will probably be ye olde Frenche lorrie drivers burning some sheep. Whatever the country, however, the one thing you can guarantee is that the outfits will be very, very silly. This part can actually be good for a laugh (or, in France, a 'lurf').

Drama School Kids. At some point the ceremony will have a large bunch of kids running around to form a pretty pattern on the field. If you are really unlucky they'll sing a song about being the future/welcoming everybody/joining the world in peace and harmony like some revolting Michael Jackson video. Obviously we at Channel Nutty think that world peace etc. are all Jolly Good Things. It's just that all the kids they pick look like they've fallen off a cola advert. They all have big white teeth and cheesy grins and WE HATE THEM! Of course it can be good fun if it rains on the little tykes … heh, heh, heh!

Naturally, the evil weevils behind the scenes keep the worst for last: **the song.**

Every opening ceremony gets a famous bod from the pop world to warble a specially written ditty to celebrate the occasion. This would be perfectly acceptable if they EVER used anyone half-way decent. Do they ask The Prodigy, Oasis or The Fun Loving Criminals to open proceedings? No, they do not. They ask Cliff Richard, Mariah Carey, Placido Domingo, Phil Collins or some other appalling old 'singer' who not even your mum likes! Even worse, as the '98 finals are in France it will probably be a French pop star, perhaps Johnny Halliday, doing the honours. What, you mean you've never heard of a French pop star? We rest our case. One solution is to wait for the song, turn the TV sound down and whack on a song of your choice at full volume. If you're in the stadium, make sure you're wearing a powerful Walkman.

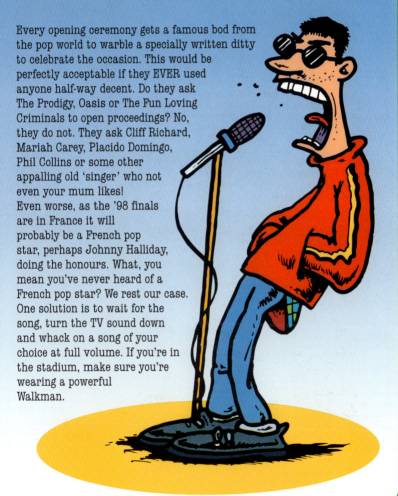

The CHANNEL NUTTY

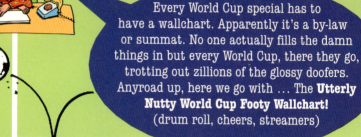

Every World Cup special has to have a wallchart. Apparently it's a by-law or summat. No one actually fills the damn things in but every World Cup, there they go, trotting out zillions of the glossy doofers. Anyroad up, here we go with … The **Utterly Nutty World Cup Footy Wallchart!**
(drum roll, cheers, streamers)

Brazil

PREDICTION:

Winners 1958,1962,1970,1994.
Kit: Yellow shirts with green trim, blue shorts, white socks.
Nutty points to look out for:
Because Brazil are usually ace, commentators go bonkers in the nut whenever a Brazilian player does anything, even taking a throw in. Keep an ear open for the following phrases:'silky skills', 'Oh I say! Only Brazil could do that!', 'samba', 'carnival atmosphere', 'Rio'.

FINISHING POSITION:

Germany

PREDICTION:

Winners 1954, 1974, 1990.
Kit: White shirts, black shorts, white socks.
Not much nuttiness about this lot. In fact they have an irritating habit of either winning the cup or losing in the finals. Just when you think they've blown it, up pops some beefy Bavarian to tonk one in the back of the net. They do have a few well dodgy haircuts however.

FINISHING POSITION:

Italy

PREDICTION:

Winners 1934, 1938,1982.
Kit: Blue shirts, white shorts, blue socks.
With a World Cup record to match Brazil's, Italy are another side who tend to keep their best for the finals. If Italy are knocked out, one thing that can be v. v. funny is to have a good laff at their sunglass-clad supporters who think they are SO cooool!

FINISHING POSITION:

France

PREDICTION:

Never won (heh, heh, heh).
Kit: Blue shirts, white shorts, red socks.
France usually look like they're going to win the competition but tend to fade away when push comes to shove. Having dropped Cantona they have a v. low Nutty Factor.

FINISHING POSITION:

Argentina

PREDICTION:

Winners 1978.
Kit: Light blue and white striped shirts, black shorts, white socks.

In 1986 nutball, Diego Maradona made us cry by punching the ball into England's net. How we laughed when four years later we saw a whole team of weeping Argentinians when they were beaten in the 1990 final! Diego made his final World Cup appearance in USA '94 when he treated us to some great goals and after he scored against Greece, running over to the camera to show us this truly frightening gob (see pic).

FINISHING POSITION:

England

PREDICTION:

Winners 1966 ('Some people are on the pitch! They think it's all over! It is now!').
Kit: White shirts, blue shorts, white socks.

With Gazza likely to be in the team, nuttiness can not be too far away. However in recent years England have looked amazingly good, with nuttiness something of a rarity. Past nuttiness includes the Gazza blub (1990), the Gazza silly face during the national anthem (any year really), Ray Wilkins chucking the ball at the ref (1986), Bobby Moore getting arrested for shoplifting (1970), Nobby Stiles (just for being called 'Nobby', 1966).

FINISHING POSITION:

Spain

PREDICTION:

Never won.
Kit: Red shirts, blue shorts, black and yellow socks.

Nowt to report on the nutty front. Spain are a tidy side who are usually tipped to be a decent bet for the World Cup but who somehow never seem to get it right on the night. Keep your eyes open for Manolo, a fanatical Spaniard who takes a MASSIVE drum to every game. Even if you can't see him you will definitely hear him!

FINISHING POSITION:

Holland

PREDICTION:

Never won.
Kit: Orange shirts, black shorts, orange socks.

Usually the Dutch play some fantastic footy at World Cups without actually winning it. In 1974 and 1978 they lost in the finals. In 1974 they took the lead without any opposing German player touching the ball! They are also good value for moaning amongst themselves. Ruud Gullit famously did this in 1994 by leaving the team and returning to Holland! Watch out for Arsenal's Dennis Bergkamp.

FINISHING POSITION:

Denmark

PREDICTION:

Never won.
Kit: Red shirts, white shorts, red socks.

With the magnificently miserable Peter Schmeichel in goal there is always a chance of nuttiness from this otherwise boringly normal team. If Denmark need a goal late on, expect to see 'Rudolph' legging it into the opponent's goalmouth.

FINISHING POSITION:

Austria

PREDICTION:

Never won.
Kit: White shirts, black shorts, black socks.

Austria are something of a non-nutty zone. Unless of course they play in the kit we've sneaked a peek at (see picture of lederhosen kit). Austria do have the novelty value of having actually been beaten 1-0 by the microscopic Faroe Islands! They don't have any famous players.

FINISHING POSITION:

Scotland

PREDICTION:

Never won.
Kit: Dark blue shirts, white shorts, blue socks.

Scotland do have a fairly nutty World Cup history. Notable moments include losing to the deeply unfancied Costa Rica in 1990; drawing with Iran in 1974 and in 1978 thousands of Scots actually listened when their manager, Ally McCleod, told a nation: 'We are going to win the World Cup.' Nutty scholars could also point to an honourable history of players with no teeth: Joe Jordan, Craig Burley, David Hopkin, Jim Leighton (see pic).

FINISHING POSITION:

Morocco

PREDICTION:

Never won.
Kit: All red.

Morocco led the African influence on the World Cup by qualifying and doing better than expected in 1970. They qualified again in 1986 and won their group (which included England, Poland and Portugal!) before going out to eventual runners up Germany. So, no mugs. As for nuttiness? Forget it.

FINISHING POSITION:

Bulgaria

PREDICTION:

Never won.
Kit: Blue shirts, red shorts, yellow socks

Quite good nutty value in recent World Cups. In addition to being quite good, they have the wonderfully angry and unpleasant Hristo Stoichkov, the goalie who got a hair transplant for the 1994 finals, and they are named after a children's TV puppet.

FINISHING POSITION:

Nigeria

PREDICTION:

Never won.
Kit: Green shirts, white shorts, green socks.

The Nigerians made an impact on the 1994 finals, getting through to the second round. They achieved instant nutty status with their amazing after-goal celebration (see 'The Euro Nutty Footy Book') where the scorer cocks his leg against the goal post as if he is a dog, erm, having a pee! Their midfield general is called Sunday …

FINISHING POSITION:

Romania

PREDICTION:

Never won.

Kit: Yellow shirts, blue shorts, red socks.

The dark horses of the championships (why 'dark' horses?) Romania are currently ranked 5th in the world FIFA tables, two places above England and could sneak into the finals. Their fantastic captain Gheorghe Hagi ('He's got a great left foot. He could open a can of beans with that foot.' Ray Clemence talking about Hagi in the '94 finals.) is their main threat alongside Chelsea's Dan Petrescu. As far as nuttiness goes they can point to the nutty fact that their first World Cup team of 1930 was picked by the King of Romania, King CAROL!

FINISHING POSITION:

Norway

PREDICTION:

Never won.

Kit: Red shirts, white shorts, blue socks.

The best thing about Norway is that you can make fun of their accent, which is kind of nutty sounding. Also they do have quite funny names: keep a look out for Man Utd's Henning Berg, Chelsea's Tor Andre Flo, Middlesbrough's Jan Aage Fjortoft. Oh, and they play horrible footy.

FINISHING POSITION:

Japan

PREDICTION:

First timers.

Kit: White shirts, red shorts, white socks.

The titchy Japanese team have made big improvements in recent years but will probably not progress. On the nutty front, watch out for a size mismatch if they play the hulking Norwegians or Nigerians ...

FINISHING POSITION:

South Africa

PREDICTION:

First timers.

KIt: Yellow and green shirts, green shorts, yellow and green socks.

The Lions of Africa are thought by some people to be capable of making a splash at their first-ever World Cup. We say: fuggetabout it! Let's face it, their number one striker is Phil Masinga, ex-Leeds United, who wasn't exactly free scoring ...

FINISHING POSITION:

Tunisia

Never won.

Kit: Red shirts, white shorts, red socks.

PREDICTION:

Pretty good side who caused a few raised eyebrows on their World Cup debut in 1978 when they beat Mexico 3-1, and drew 1-1 with reigning champs, West Germany. No nutty qualities at all I'm afraid.

FINISHING POSITION:

Jamaica

PREDICTION:

First timers.

Kit: Green shirts, black shorts, gold socks.

Jamaica have done brill just to qualify and we can expect a certain level of laid-back nuttiness from both team and supporters. Example: when they score the RastaBoyz (the Jamaican equivalent of Scotland's Tartan Army) don't sing 'You're not singing any more ...' They chant 'I an' I will praise Jah for smitin' the Babylon raas claat. Together we shall prevail. Together we shall prevail ...'

FINISHING POSITION:

Chile

Never won.

PREDICTION:

Kit: Red and white shirts, blue shorts, white socks.

The South Americans used to have a fair chance in the finals, qualifying in 1930, 1950 and hosting it in 1962 when they finished 3rd. However they have not done much since. In the past, however, Chile have proved to be capable of mucho nuttino. In 1990 they were banned by FIFA from the World Cup after their captain PRETENDED he had been injured by a missile during a qualifier against Brazil! (see: 'The Nutty Footy Book', page 80)

FINISHING POSITION:

Cameroon

Never won.

kit: Green shirts, red shorts, yellow socks.

PREDICTION:

The 1990 Cameroon team surprised everyone by actually being very good! They were only knocked out 3-2 by England at the quarter-final stage.

Could be some nutty moments ahead after their coach, Henri Depireux, quit because he hadn't been paid! They have a player called R. Song; this means that the commentator may well say, 'They're playing R. Song.'!

FINISHING POSITION:

United States

PREDICTION:

Never won.

Kit: White shirts, blue shorts, red socks.

Having been in the finals in 1990 and 1994 the US are getting quite used to the top flight and have caused some great upsets in the past (see page 31). We're looking forward to the match with Iran (OUCH!) and the appearance of The Bearded One (Alexei Lalas).

FINISHING POSITION:

South Korea

Never won.

Kit: All red.

PREDICTION:

Last seen in World Cup 1990, the South Koreans almost upset West Germany before being dumped out in round 1. Main source of nuttiness comes from the possibility of them having very funny names.

FINISHING POSITION:

Mexico

PREDICTION:

Never won.

Kit: Green shirts, white shorts, red socks.

Best showing: two quarter-final slots. Best chance of nuttiness: if the goalie designs his own kit like he did in 1986 (see page 17).

FINISHING POSITION:

Belgium
Never won.
Kit: All red with tricolour trim.

PREDICTION:

The plucky Belgians have done pretty well in various World Cups, including a semi-final spot in 1986. However we still can't think of more than three famous Belgians (Phillippe Albert, Enzo Schifo and Hercule Poirot) and one of them isn't real.

FINISHING POSITION:

Paraguay
Never won.
Kit: Red and white shirts, blue shorts and socks.

PREDICTION:

Not a bad record for a side usually considered to be one of South America's weakest. They've played in 3, including the first. An unknown quantity as far as nuttiness is concerned.

FINISHING POSITION:

Saudi Arabia
Never won.
Kit: All white with green trim.

PREDICTION:

Nothing to report on the desert warriors except that they looked darned good last time, making excellent teams work very hard. No nuttiness expected.

FINISHING POSITION:

Iran
Never won.

PREDICTION:

Kit: Green shirts, white shorts, red socks.
The Iranians famously knocked out Terry Venables' Australians to qualify and were then drawn to play their sworn enemies, the USA! Could be a teensy bit of needle in that one ...

FINISHING POSITION:

Colombia
Never won.
Kit: Red shirts with tricolour trim, blue shorts and red socks with tricolour trim.

PREDICTION:

Colombia are famous for having the magnificently nutty Rene Higueta in goal (see page 16) and the brilliantly bouffanted Carlos Valderramma (see page 15) and for having a player shot dead after scoring an own goal in 1994. Top nutters.

FINISHING POSITION:

Croatia
Never won.

PREDICTION:

Kit: Red/white shirts, red/white shorts, white socks.
Croatia don't have a great nutty pedigree but as far as footy goes they could cause a few World Cup ripples. With top players like Alen Boksiz and Davor Suker experienced in the Spanish and Italian leagues, Croatia are a good outside bet.

FINISHING POSITION:

Yugoslavia
Never won.

PREDICTION:

Kit: Blue shirts, white shorts, red socks.
Yugoslavia have a good World Cup past without actually getting to the finals itself. Watch out for fireworks if they draw Croatia in the later rounds ...

FINISHING POSITION:

Other channels bring you the usual guff about the great players: Pele, Beckenbauer, Cruyff. We like to dig out the nuttier side of things, so here is our personal collection of nutty World Cup greats to cut out and keep ... in our **All Time Nutter Eleven.**

No.1 Peter Schmeichel. Denmark.

The Great Dane is well known to Channel Nutty viewers. Who can forget the sight of Old Red Nose nodding home a goal against Rotor Volvograd or some such ridiculous East European club? Whatever happens, he can be relied on to maintain his impressively high Nutty Factor.

No.2 Ruud Gullit. Holland.

Ruud is mainly included for his fantastically nutty hairdo and his name which is filled with nutty possibilities. He's also there for his ability to whinge like nobody's business. In his last World Cup campaign for Holland, Ruud left early when he disagreed with the team the manager picked! He wasn't alone though; the Dutch team have a proud tradition of flouncing out of World Cups...

No.3 Stuart Pearce. England.

In 1990 this dependable England full back sliced his cosmically important semi-final penalty wide and shattered a nation's hopes. Fast forward to 1996 and incredibly Stu (and us) are in the same position again! Who can forget the insane gob on 'Psycho' Stu Pearce after he slotted his penalty decider against Spain? Well, I can't, anyway.

No.4 Hristo Stoichkov. Bulgaria.

Old Hristo is undoubtedly one of the game's great footballing fellers. However it's not his pace, power or skill which makes him a Channel Nutty great. It is his amazingly miserable gob. We think he has to be related to Mancunian songster, Morrisey, such is Hristo's capacity to be sour, unhappy and, let's be honest, rather nasty.

No.5 Alexei Lalas. USA.

Cannot be mistaken for anyone else. Alexei burst into the big time during the USA's 1994 World Cup campaign and is in our all time eleven on the strength of his flame red BEARD and straggly rock star haircut!

WORLD CUP GREATS

No.6 Nobby Stiles. England.

Picked for having the name 'Nobby', Stiles made a huge impact on the 1966 World Cup. He was actually in the winning team! This is hard to credit when you see what a scruffy little toothless Scouser old Nobby was. Will be remembered for his lunatic dancing on the 1966 lap of honour*.

No.7 Eric Cantona. France.

In any team of nutters, Eric has to be given a place. Nutty highlights: kung fuing a Crystal Palace yobbo, hoicking his collar up, strutting around after scoring, and spouting complete rubbish at press conferences ('When seagulls follow the trawler it is because they expect sardines.').

No.8 Attilio Lombardo. Italy.

At Nutty Footy we are honoured to salute one of the few genuine slapheads to walk tall, bald and proud in the world game. Attilio 'The Mekon' Lombardo, apart from being an ACE footy player is renowned to have insisted on a maid, butler, Rolls Royce and mansion on top of his wages when he joined Crystal Palace!

No.9 Paul Gascoigne. England.

Gazza needs no introduction to regular Channel Nutty viewers. He has probably been responsible for more genuinely nutty moments in footy history than any player since Willie 'Fatty' Foulkes back in the twenties. A genuinely ace player, you can always rely on Gazza to do the wrong thing at the right time. Or the right thing at the wrong time. Or summat …

No.10 Carlos Valderrama. Colombia.

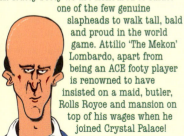

Valderrama is included in the line up not for his silky skills but for his top-class nutty hair! Just get a load of that bonce!

No.11 Jurgen Klinsmann. Germany.

Jurgen is in the Nutty Greats not for his footy skills which are beyond question, but for his large collection of European currency. 'Klinky' has perfected the art of smelling a fast buck in a glittering footy career which has seen him chasing medals at Spurs, Bayern Munich, Samdoria and, er Spurs again …

*see THE UTTERLY NUTTY HISTORY OF FOOTY, page 39.

The Nutty World Of ... GOALIES

We **love** goalies on Channel Nutty. Why? Because (a) they are nutty before they even get on to the pitch, (b) they do incredibly nutty stuff when they're on the pitch and (c) because they can liven up the **dullest** World Cup tie!

Take the Bulgarian keeper, **Boris Mikhailov**, who played the qualifying rounds of the 1994 World Cup as a baldie but who then turned up for the tournament with a full head of hair! His wig escaped during a goalmouth incident and Boris had to chase it round the pitch (we made that bit up 'cos it was an excuse for a funny picture!). Boris had actually had an Elton John style full hair transplant!

Shaggy-haired Colombian keeper **Rene Higueta** had no such problems. The ringleted nutter is most famous for this astonishing save during a match against England in 1995! Rene is also noted for getting bored in goal and dribbling the length of the pitch. More than once this has cost Colombia a goal. In the 1990 World Cup Rene set off on a run only for Cameroon striker Roger Millar to rob him and slide the ball into the empty net!

Mighty Irish keeper **Pat Jennings** won a record 119th cap during the 1986 World Cup. Pat was noted for his giant mitts which were known, rather boringly, as 'The Largest Hands In Soccer'. Here's a picture using a full-size ball to give you an idea of the problems strikers had scoring past Pat!

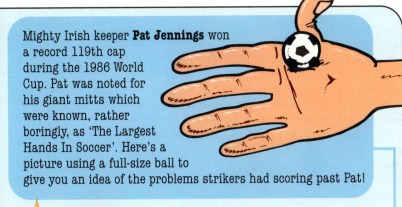

Mexico's keeper during the 1994 World Cup had a lot to answer for. He turned out in the most SPECTACULARLY VILE shirt (yes, worse than David Seaman's infamous 'explosion in a paint factory' shirt) ever seen on a footy pitch. What made this disgusting object even more unforgivable was that the goalie had designed it himself!

Lev Yashin was the popular Russian goalie who played in the 1958, 1962 and 1966 World Cups. Dressed from head to toe in black, Lev's nickname was 'The Black Octopus'...

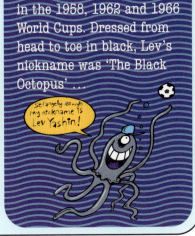

strangely enough my nickname is Lev Yashin!

England's 1966 World Cup winning keeper, **Gordon Banks**, famous for his astonishing acrobatic 1970 World Cup save against the great Brazilian, Pele, finished his career with only ONE eye! After losing it in a car crash, Gordon continued playing footy for two more seasons in the USA!

New Nutty World Cup

RULES

Before the start of the 1994 competition, which was held in the USA, there was a lot of silly loose talk about FIFA making changes to the beautiful game (that's 'football' to those of you supporting Leeds) to make it more acceptable to namby-pamby American audiences who thought footy was too boring. Americans like action! thrills! complicated rules! more equipment! more goals! One suggestion was to make the goals wider as the game went on. Another was to take players off one by one if the score was goalless. Other thoughts included getting rid of the offside rule, putting a second ref on the pitch, punishing players by putting them in a 'sin-bin', etc. etc. In the European Championships in 1996 one of the suggestions was actually used. 'Sudden Death' was used during England's semi-final against Germany, with the winner in extra time being the first side to score. And, it has to be said, it was very, very exciting and scary.

With the added excitement in mind, we actually think that rule changes could be a Dead Good Thing. So here are a few of Channel Nutty's new rules ...

1. More Danger. Nothing makes players sit up and take notice as much as a bit of real danger. We suggest concealed water hazards being revealed as the game progresses. Crocodiles, sharks and piranha fish can be added according to the referee's wishes.

2. Big Boxes. To add to the number of goalmouth incidents, we suggest simply making the penalty box much bigger, say to about the half-way line. This would mean that most of the game would be played in the box and Jimmy Hill, Barry Davies and Alan Hansen could STOP MOANING!

3. Titchy Goalies. If a match remains goalless after ninety minutes then teams must play a person of limited stature between the sticks for the extra-time period. Outfield pint-sizes like Gianfranco Zola or Dennis Wise would not be allowed to don the gloves.

4. Instant Winter. With World Cups almost always being played in hot countries during the summer, it can be hard to remember sometimes just what it's like to be up to your armpits in freezing mud and snow. Not only that, it's very unfair to the Northern European sides to be playing in 130-degree heat. Think about it, would Brazil be as succesful if the tournament was held in Norway in November? I think not! Our patented 'Instant Winter' apparatus would be installed at all World Cup venues. In a microsecond the match officials could change the weather conditions, altering, for example, Dallas to Darlington!

5. Commentator Substitutions.

This rule would come into effect whenever a commentator makes a particularly cretinous remark. For example, when Barry Davies starts to whine like some demented school teacher about a player making the wrong pass/shot/header, the TV audience, via specially adapted remote controls, can 'zap' the commentator on to the field of play to see exactly how Barry would do it!

6. Transformobots. Specially trained and biologically altered players who can transform themselves, into lethal indestructible cartoon fighting machines with special powers. These Transformobots can be used during extra-time periods to ginger up the opposition. (Obviously David Batty is already a Transformobot and is exempt from the 'extra time only' rule.) Pictured is Steve McManaman in the process of turning into 'SkullBot, Emperor and Ultimate Lord of the Ninth Ring of Uranus', sworn to wreak havoc across the universe!

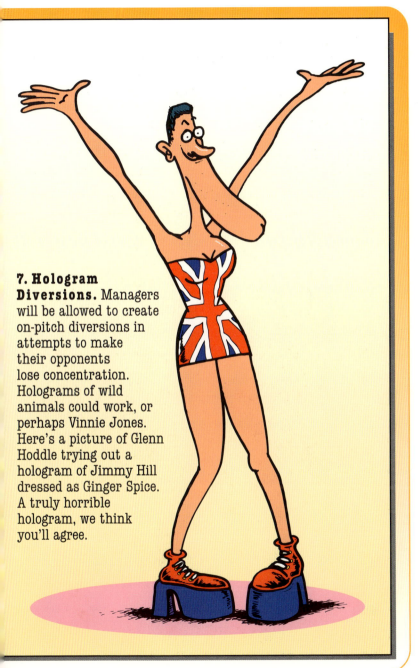

7. Hologram Diversions. Managers will be allowed to create on-pitch diversions in attempts to make their opponents lose concentration. Holograms of wild animals could work, or perhaps Vinnie Jones. Here's a picture of Glenn Hoddle trying out a hologram of Jimmy Hill dressed as Ginger Spice. A truly horrible hologram, we think you'll agree.

Nutty World Cup

FACTS

We all know that sometimes footy matches can be bad-tempered affairs. But in 1970 the qualifying matches for the Mexico World Cup between El Salvador and Honduras resulted in WAR between the two countries! After three games filled with bad feeling and tension, the fourth game triggered an attack by El Salvador on the airport at Tegucigalpa in Honduras ...

In qualifying, El Salvador had to put up with a witch doctor from Haiti sprinkling voodoo powder on the pitch before the game in Haiti! El Salvador coach Gregorio Bundio was obviously not too superstitious: he punched the witch doctor, knocking him out cold when the teams met for the return leg!

Let's face it, all of us know that referees are, quite simply, a few sandwiches short of a picnic. Proof, if proof were needed, comes in the shape of 1966 World Cup referee George McCabe who changed the name of his house to 'Jules Rimet', after the famous World Cup trophy!

The atmosphere for the 1950 World Cup final played in Rio de Janeiro between Brazil and Uruguay must have been quite something. A record 199,854 people attended the match at the famous Maracana Stadium!

On the subject of referees, the 1958 World Cup had a referee no one could argue with. His name? Edward Faultless ...

Italy 0 Diddy Men 1

In 1966 North Korea qualified for the first time ever for the World Cup finals. Based on Merseyside for the competition, the short (none of the team was taller than 5 ft 8 inches) North Koreans were nicknamed 'The Diddymen' after toothy, local comedian, Ken Dodd's TV characters. Following a defeat against the Soviet Union and a draw against Chile, the 'Diddymen' stunned world football by notching up a shock 1-0 victory against the mighty Italians, knocking them out of the competition!

Woodenspoon
Italy '66

World Cup Legends Appear in Rubbish Film Shock! Yes, in 1981 one of the very worst (and, one of the very funniest) films ever made starred World Cup heroes Pele (Brazil), Ossie Ardiles (Argentina) and Bobby Moore (England)! Set during the Second World War, 'Escape to Victory' concerned the exploits of a team of footballing prisoners of war. The team included the astonishing sight of SYLVESTER STALLONE (!) playing alongside the real footy stars with a very tubby Michael Caine also in the line up! During an enthralling match they plan to escape through a tunnel below the team bath(!) at half time, however they return to the pitch to trounce the Nazi scum ...

When Scotland travelled to play Estonia it's fair to say that most of the Scottish players had only a sketchy idea of where Estonia actually was. However, it appears that even the Estonian players weren't too sure either, as they failed to turn up for the crucial World Cup qualifier! Scottish supporters were treated to the nutty sight of Scotland kicking off with no opposition on the field! The match lasted all of ten seconds. FIFA ordered the game to be replayed and thankfully Scotland won.

Scotland do set very high standards for their players. Henry Morris played his first game for Scotland in the 1949 World Cup qualifier against Northern Ireland. The Scots walloped the Irish 8-2 and Henry notched an impressive hat trick, scoring the first ever World Cup goal by a British player. The result? Morris was never picked to play for Scotland again!

Nutty World Cup Quiz

Get your anoraks out, because it's time to test your World Cup knowledge in our fiendishly difficult quiz-type thing ...

 1 Which pony-tailed Italian Buddhist missed the final penalty of the 1994 World Cup?

 2 Which jug-eared crisp flogger scored the most goals in the 1990 World Cup tournament?

 3 Against which team did Bryan 'Captain Marvel' Robson score England's quickest-ever World Cup goal in just 27 seconds?

 4 Which side did the ancient Roger Milla play for in the 1990 World Cup?

 5 In the 1990 World Cup one player committed more fouls than any other. He is currently managing a side who just failed to qualify for World Cup 1998. Who is he and who does he manage?

 6 England manager, Glenn Hoddle, has an embarrassing nickname. What is it?

7 How many World Cups did dodgy, diddy, digit diddler, Diego Maradona play in?

 8 Gary Lineker scored 48 goals for England, one under the record of 49. Which baldie Red Devil holds that record?

 9 What was the name of the black and white dog who found the World Cup trophy after it had been nicked in 1966?

 10 When Daniel Xuereb played for France in the 1986 World Cup it meant that a complete A to Z of players had competed in the tournament down the years. True or false?

Answers: 1-Roberto Baggio. 2-Gary Lineker. 3-France. 4-Cameroon. 5-Mick McCarthy, Republic of Ireland. 6-Glenda. 7-4. 8-Bobby Charlton. 9-Pickles. 10-True.

Scores:

1–3 Why are you doing this quiz? Did your mother drop you on your head as a baby? You know less about footy than a hideous blend of Jimmy Hill and Trevor Francis. Leave now and spend the rest of the year in a Football Monastery where you will have time to reflect on your shameful ignorance!

4–7 Better, but still room for improvement. It's not as though we asked any really obscure or difficult questions, is it?

8–10 OO-ER! State of you! I suppose you think you know it all now, don't you? Actually you probably do; would you like a job?

Classic World Cup
COMMENTATING NONSENSE

'My legs sort of disappeared from nowhere.'

Chris Waddle talking about his 1990 semi-final penalty miss.

'The World Cup – truly an international event.'

John Motson

'He's got two feet has Zola.'

David Pleat

'Playing with wingers is more effective against European sides like Brazil than English sides like Wales.'

Ron Greenwood

'I don't think there is anyone bigger or smaller than Maradona.'

Kevin Keegan

'Someone in the England team will have to grab the ball by the horns.'

Ron Atkinson

'On the pitch the Italians looked no different to us. It was like playing Bournemouth on a wet Saturday.'

Jason McAteer after playing for Ireland in their 1994 World Cup win over Italy.

'A film called Passport To Terror will follow and I think this referee will be in it.'

GIBBER

Des Lynam talking about referee Jamal Al-Sharif who went card crazy in the 1994 Bulgaria v. Mexico game.

'God is a Bulgarian.'

Nutty Bulgarian, Hristo Stoichkov after his team won in the same game.

'God is still a Bulgarian, but the referee was French.'

Stoichkov after defeat in Bulgaria's next game against Italy

YAK

BLAH

'There were three countries in the world that would have caused us problems, so we're very pleased they won't be coming: Iran, Iraq and England.'

Alan Rothenberg, 1994 USA World Cup chairman

'If I played for Scotland my grandma would be the proudest woman in the country – if she wasn't dead.'

Mark Crossley

'The England manager has a choice of Gascoigne, Platt, Beardsley and Ince. Any of those would be in the Swiss side. I've got to pick between Sforza, Sforza and Sforza. I usually pick Sforza.'

Roy Hodgson when manager of Switzerland

'If people saw me walking on water you can be sure someone would say: "Look at that Bertie Vogts, he can't even swim."'

Bertie Vogts, German coach

One HIT Wonders

A nutty guide to those teams that have made brief but memorable appearances in the World Cup Finals.

These days you'll hear managers spouting off about how there are no real pushover opponents in world football. And, those of us who remember England when Graham Taylor was the manager, might agree. In 1993 a part-time pizza chef called Galtieri scored the quickest-ever World Cup goal after EIGHT seconds against England for the incredibly titchy San Marino. It was their first-ever World Cup goal and, although England recovered to win 7-1, it is the San Marino goal which is remembered.

However, that was in the qualifying rounds, where the likes of San Marino, the Faroe Isles, Luxembourg and Wales (only kidding, lovely Welsh readers!) at least get to play against the big boys. By the time we reach the actual World Cup most of the real minnows have been knocked out. Over the years there have been a number of great performances by unfancied sides in the tournament and some great nutty moments ...

Zaire 1974

Zaire had a difficult World Cup. 3-0 down to Yugoslavia after 22 minutes the manager had a brainwave. He would take off his useless keeper Muamba Kazadi. Things immediately looked up ... for Yugoslavia, who promptly slotted another SIX goals past substitute keeper Dimbi Tubilandu! In another game a Zairean defender, lining up in a defensive wall, lost his mind and, before the free kick had been taken, broke from the wall to welly the ball upfield! He was sent off ...

Kuwait 1982

After qualifying for the 1982 World Cup the Kuwaiti side lost its three games, although England only beat them 1-0. However, in a game against host nations France, a truly nutty scene took place. After a whistle was blown in the crowd the Kuwaiti players stopped and France scored! The outraged Kuwaiti king came down from the stands and ordered his team off the pitch in protest! They eventually returned to lose 4-1.

Haiti 1974

In order to qualify for the finals tiny Haiti mysteriously were given permission to play ALL their games at home! As if this wasn't advantage enough, referees tended to disallow any goals scored against Haiti, including FOUR scored by Trinidad! When they did get to the finals their centre half failed a drug test, the team bodyguards beat up members of the Haiti team and then kidnapped a German FIFA official plus a Polish journalist!

USA 1950

Since the USA have played in four World Cups they are not strictly speaking 'one-hit wonders' either. However in 1950 they stunned the football world by beating England 1-0. Back then the USA had no league to speak of and they had not had to qualify for the tournament. England were widely tipped as possible world champions. However in the game itself the ball would not go in the American net, hitting the woodwork 12 times! In contrast US striker Larry Gaetjens headed what amounted to the only American effort on goal and it went in ...

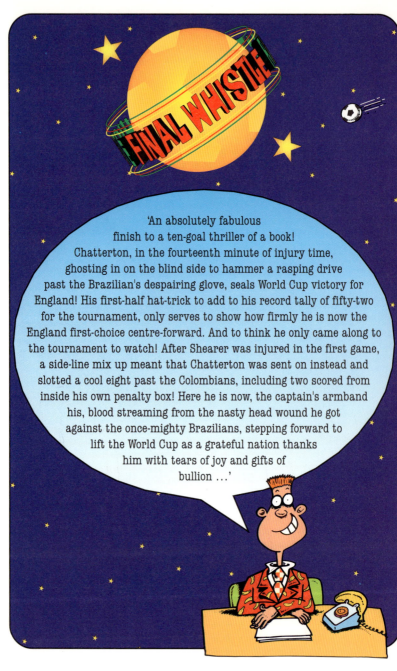

'An absolutely fabulous finish to a ten-goal thriller of a book! Chatterton, in the fourteenth minute of injury time, ghosting in on the blind side to hammer a rasping drive past the Brazilian's despairing glove, seals World Cup victory for England! His first-half hat-trick to add to his record tally of fifty-two for the tournament, only serves to show how firmly he is now the England first-choice centre-forward. And to think he only came along to the tournament to watch! After Shearer was injured in the first game, a side-line mix up meant that Chatterton was sent on instead and slotted a cool eight past the Colombians, including two scored from inside his own penalty box! Here he is now, the captain's armband his, blood streaming from the nasty head wound he got against the once-mighty Brazilians, stepping forward to lift the World Cup as a grateful nation thanks him with tears of joy and gifts of bullion ...'